Love Letters to a Home

AF624607

Mairead Dunsmore

BookLeaf Publishing

Presentation by *BookLeaf Publishing*

Web: www.bookleafpub.com

E-mail: info@bookleafpub.com

ISBN: 978-93-95784-95-5

First edition 2022

Selfishly I'm dedicating this one to myself.

I didn't think I could do it, but I have, and now it's done.

ACKNOWLEDGEMENT

I'd like to take this little bit of time to thank my family, who not only have helped me clear out my house and take mountains of boxes to the dump, but who have also met me for coffee when I needed to get out of the house and listened to me when I ranted about contractors.

I also want to thank my friends who have done lots of little tasks around my new house, especially Ellie and Niamh who chipped paint off of my doorframes and came to paint for me when I asked. I can't understate how much I am thankful to know you.

What makes a home, I wonder?

What makes a home, I wonder?

I'm asking cause I need to know,
Pictures on the wall? Well I have zero.
My walls don't even have paint.

I've just moved and my home is bare.
I have no space to move but boxes to spare. But
no cupboards to unpack them into.

We bought a fixer upper, a place to fill,
With ideas of a home that I have still,
Yet I have no energy to work.

Cause a house of your own, now that's the
dream,
It once was mine but now I just scream,
If I think about drilling another hole.

I've sanded, and tidied, and painted away,
But my list gets longer not shorter every day,
And I don't think it will ever end.

And the problem I've found, which angers me so,
Is that each project I start, I've another to go,
So I can't ever picture the end.

Is this being an adult now, I ask?
Cause every day I'm facing an impossible task,
One that has no clear finish in sight.

Yes the impossible task, I've been told that's the way.
That when you've grown up all the others will say,
That work stops coming in neat little packages.

Now when you finish one bit and leave it behind,
It doesn't disappear it just bides it's time,
Until it rears its ugly head again.

The problem is now that I have to learn,
To not dread the day that the task returns,
But to put it to the back of my mind.

But I'm a thinker, a planner; I'm a panicker,
I don't know how to ignore a challenger,
This task that I need to complete.

So when the night comes, and I go to bed,

I just think of all the tasks that I dread,
The worry can't go into a cardboard box.

So I ask all my friends with a fake little smile,
Will you carry my burdens with me for a while?
But they are too busy carrying their own.

I turn to my family, my siblings, my blood,
I ask them will you help me weather this flood?
And they tell me they have to deal with theirs
first.

Is this being an adult now, I wonder?
Will no one come and offer me cover,
Do I have to face all trials on my own?

So yes I ask, but no one comes running,
The house stands with just me, all others are
shunning,
The cry for help that I'm putting out.

So I wake up each morning, and face my
despair,
I pick up paintbrush and alone I stand there,
Becoming a woman with no one to see.

What makes a home, I wonder?
Is it the feeling of safety I've yet to discover,
A place where I feel most loved.

Cause the way the house is, how it makes me so lonely,
I'm starting to wonder if it will ever feel homely,
With just me to fix it right up.

Colour

I'm painting my living room yellow,
Happy and comfy and mellow,
To make me feel gleeful,
When I'm feeling quite tearful,
What makes me happy? It's yellow.

I'm painting my hallway sage green,
Welcoming and homely and keen,
To make me feel happy,
When I'm feeling quite scrappy,
What makes me happy? It's green.

I'm painting my bedroom pale blue,
Sweet and lovely and new,
To make me feel pretty,
When I'm feeling quite shitty,
What makes me happy? It's blue.

I'm ridding myself of the plaster,
Boring and dark, a disaster.
It makes me so fed up,
I wish this all sped up,
What makes me happy? Not plaster!

Sanding on the Brain

Bzzz, Bzzz, Bzzz,
I'm in a love-hate relationship with my sander.
Brrr, brrr, brrr,
It is like a boyfriend I need to put up with.

Pttt, pttt, pttt,
I love the feeling of power it gives me.
Zzzt, zzzt, zzzt,
I hate the way it sounds.

Tttp, tttp, tttp,
I hate the dust that gets everywhere.
Sssp, sssp, sssp,
I love the floor when you clean the dust away.

Pppt, pppt, pppt,
I love to be able to fix something.
Fffp, fffp, fffp,
I hate how it feels like I'm breaking it instead.

Bzzz, bzzz, bzzz,
I'm in a love-hate relationship with my sander.
Brrr, brrr, brrr,
With the headaches it gives me,
It'd better be bloody worth it.

The To-Do List of a Crazy Woman

Early morning to do list:
-Tidy up kitchen
-Make a cup of coffee
-Paint that spot in the living room
-forget about your cup of coffee
-tidy up the living room
-move your piano to the right corner
-second coat of paint on that spot in the living room
-remember your cup of coffee
-drink your cup of coffee
-hate your cup of coffee because it's cold now
-throw that cup of coffee down the drain
-be sad that you didn't enjoy your coffee
-decide to drill a hole in the wall for a shelf
-measure the spot for the shelf
-get the stud checker up
-calibrate the stud checker
-use the stud checker
-all clear, mark your holes in the wall
-drill your holes in the wall
-hit a stud on the last hole you need to drill
-be angry
-get the stud checker back out

-check for studs
-there's a stud right on that spot you tried to drill into
-be angrier
-spend ten minutes looking for the new spot for the shelf
-get fucking enraged
-cry because you are fucking enraged
-get so upset that your boyfriend leaves his office and work to come check that you are alright
-get over the hole situation
-fix the holes in the wall
-pause because you've realised that wall spot needs another coat of paint
-paint that spot
-return to the holes in the wall
-fill the holes in the wall
-wait for the filler to dry
-wait
-wait
-wait
-make a cup of tea
-wait
-time to sand the filler
-sand the filler
-paint the wall over the filler
-forget about your cup of tea
-drill the wall where the screws can actually go

-put the screws in the wall
-hang the shelf on the screws
-stand back and feel hollow inside
-realise that your shelf is squint
-realise that you couldn’t care less
-realise that you forgot about your cup of tea
-realise that the morning is over and you’ve
done absolutely nothing

Stripping Paint

Here's to the friends who come when you need,
The ones who appear to help you proceed.
I know that before them I felt so alone,
But finally they've come and I feel at home.

Here's to the friends who help you paint rooms,
The ones who arrive and good progress resumes.
I know that before them I struggled to finish,
But finally they've come and my workload's
diminished.

Here's to the friends who help you chip paint,
The ones who will do it without any complaint.
I know that before them I cracked under the
weight,
But finally they've come and my rooms are
looking great.

Here's to the friends who came when I asked,
The ones who are willing to help with this task.
I know that before them I never could thrive,
But finally they've come and I know I'll survive.

Here's to the friends who come help with my
aims
The ones whose pictures I put in all of my
frames.
I know that before them I rarely felt loved,
But finally they've come and I'll weather this
flood.

Relaxation Time

I'm lighting a candle for relaxation. It's my time right now, I finally get to relax and switch off my very busy brain.

Breathe…

The painting isn't finished,
There's one thing more to do,
All the work you've done so far is diminished,
Because here's something coming to bother you.

No, no, no. This is my time to enjoy myself. I'm making a cup of tea and turning off my head. This isn't the time to finish the painting, I can do that tomorrow. Right now is the time for me to have a break.

You could do the painting right now though,
It's just sitting there, asking to be done,
It would only take you ten minutes so,
You could do it now and have some fun.

Nope, no. Painting isn't fun, it's work and it'll take much longer than ten minutes. I'm ignoring it, I'm ignoring the rhyming scheme. I'm relaxing today so just leave me be, thank you.

Just this task is there waiting,
So just pick it up, you know how,
If you leave it to sit it will just become grating,
You'd might as well just do it right now.

I'm not doing it. I'm not. I'm not. I'm not. I'm relaxing.

But how exactly do you expect to relax?
Do it now, it just takes a little time,
You really should just face the facts,
Wanting to get it done now isn't a crime.

No, no. I'm meant to be switching off. It's my day.

But how exactly do you expect to switch off?
When there's just this little job to do,
This painting, I swear, it's just a one-off,
Then you can enjoy your relaxation too.

It might be nice actually. To complete the painting and just get it done. It's only a little thing, right? Only one tiny little thing and then I'll move on.

Exactly, just the painting and then no more.
A small task, absolutely no fuss,
Relax after, do this before,
It’s easy as anything, just listen to us.

Alright, I’ll start the painting, it won’t take me too long. I’ll just pick up a paintbrush and it’ll be finished so quickly. Then I can get to relaxing, right Task List?

Well…

I suppose there is one thing we didn’t tell you,
Just one more quick thing to do,
Then when you've done that, there's lots more behind it,
Now you're up, might as well do them too!

Tiling

I
find that
I quite enjoy
the process of tiling.
It is a very relaxing
sort of process where I get
to revel in finally finishing the puzzle.
It's simple and straightforward and always
makes sense.
If only life were as simple as
a puzzle. Where everything has an
answer that you can find
if only you look.
I have enjoyed
finishing the
tiling.

A Clean State of Mind

Dirty feet, dirty toes,
With dirty floors, that's the way it goes.

Dirty bedroom, dirty mind,
Far too dirty to just leave behind.

Dirty bathroom, dirty wall,
And now I'm having a clean withdrawal.

Dirty counters, dirty space,
Everything's dirty, it's such a disgrace.

Dirty clothes, dirty dress,
With dirt everywhere I'm in distress.

Dirty blinds, dirty windows,
I'm surrounded by dirt in this cleaning limbo.

Dirty desk, dirty doors,
I can't fix it till I've finished the floor.

Dirty garden, dirty drive,
So for now I'm just being buried alive.

Dirty couch, dirty you,
The dirt is so bad, it sticks like glue.

Dirty shower, dirty screen.
Pray for the day you can finally clean.

Dirty house, dirty home.
Just wait for the dirt to finally be gone.

How’s your spelling?

O is for:
Oh God, I’m really struggling

V is for:
Very, very, very sick of this shit

E is for:
Every day, I have the same terrible feelings.

R is for:
Run away, run away, this won’t ever get better.

W is for:
When the hell will this house finally be
finished?

H is for:
Help me, please. Anyone.

E is for:
Even my poems are stressing me out now.

L is for:
Living this way is so bad for my health.

M is for:
Me wanting to take a long walk off a short pier

E is for:
Everything is becoming really too much for me

D is for:
Do you think that I will ever stop feeling this
way?

Halfway

If I gave you half a poem,
Would that really be so bad?
All the best rhymes are in the first half,
Would that be fine or make you mad?

If I gave you half a story,
Would you scream and shout and yell?
The exciting part is the intro,
When I have no other parts to tell.

If I gave you half an idea,
Would that upset you greatly?
Cause I find I'm running out of new ones,
So could that just do you, maybe?

If I gave you half a finished report,
You'd probably be pretty angry,
Cause it would just leave you more work to do,
I think you'd rightly be annoyed at me.

If I gave you half a home to live in,
With tasks still piled high to do,
Would you find that you'd be frustrated?
Would you feel the way I do too?

Cause I find now I’ve halfway finished,
With this house, but I’ve still more to go,
But I don’t have the energy to continue,
But halfway is not complete I know.

I’ve been stuck now this house is halfway,
Though there’s only a little bit more,
But I’m begging cause I need to tell you,
I really can’t do it anymore.

So can halfway just be alright for now?
I asking please just for the freedom,
I want you to tell me that it’s okay,
I can leave it as is, it’s no problem.

OK

Ok

How is it going? I'm just checking in.
I hope it's all going great.
Is the painting alright? Is the place proving nice?
Are you settling in? Is it a state?

Is the floor still a mess? Did you remove all your rubbish?
I'm just checking in, making sure.
Is the place proving strong? Are the doors all still on?
Are you feeling safe and secure?

Did you get that shelf up? Did you hang that picture?
I'm just checking in, want to know.
Have you finished it yet? Are you almost complete?
Is your house finally ready to show?

Oh yes I suppose, I forgot to really ask, how are you doing in all this?
Oh you're feeling overwhelmed?

Oh you’re struggling a lot?
Oh that’s a shame, but just think soon you’ll be finished!

Let's Discuss

So let's discuss, what do I like so far?
What do I have to be proud of?

I'm proud of my living room, which is all
complete.
It's yellow and comfortable and sweet.
I couldn't be happier, yes there's more to do,
But I'm proud of that one space at least.

I'm happy with my tiling, which I finally
finished.
It's messy but in a cute way it's nice.
I couldn't be happier, yes there's more tiles to
do,
But I'm proud of that one spot, at least.

I like my hallway, which is nearly done.
It's painted, just the floors left to do.
I couldn't be happier, although I know it's not
finished,
But I'm proud of that one bit, at least.

I don't hate myself, which is something.
It goes back and forth though I'll tell you.

I could be happier, but some days I manage so
I'll say:
I'm proud of that one part, at least.

Just Right

My radiators are too big.

My holes are always drilled too small.

My door handles are too high,

My bathroom ceiling is too low.

My shelf needs to move one inch to the right.

My shelf needs to move one inch to the left.

But once all that is fixed.
Once that's all done,
It'll be just right.

Shock

It's always shock, that's always true,
When they look up and down and say 'really you?'
Yes I am doing the construction, yes it is only me,
No boyfriend to do it, no one else, you see?

It's always shock, it's always the case,
When they see I'm a woman and surprise hits their face,
Yes I learned how to do it, yes I can manage,
I don't need your help, I have no disadvantage.

It's always shock, I can always see,
How they'll talk to my Dad but they won't talk to me.
Yes I am a person, yes I'm standing right here,
But they make me feel like I should just disappear.

It's always shock, it's always in their eyes,
I can see the present worry that they can't disguise.
Yes I am very young, yes I don't look strong,
But I know I can do it, I will prove them wrong.

It's always shock, it's always right there,
It's why I hate contractors, that judging stare.
Yes somehow I know it, yes somehow I can,
It's really a miracle how I can do things like a man.

It's always shock, and I hate it I swear,
They claim they aren't sexist but the assumptions are there.
Yes somehow I'll make it, yes somehow it'll get done,
Somehow I will manage it even though I'm a woman.

Not A Surprise

I cried again yesterday.
Not a surprise.
I spilled paint on my car,
I spilled tears in my eyes.
I thought it was ruined,
I thought I'd destroyed it,
But when the tears were gone,
It was just paint on a carpet.

I freaked out again last week,
Not a surprise.
I broke one of my new dishes,
I broke my feeling of pride.
I thought it was awful,
I thought I wouldn't recover,
But I brushed it away,
And bought myself another.

I got upset again today,
Not a surprise,
I gave more than I could manage,
I gave less than I could provide.
I thought I was the worst,
I thought I was the problem,

But I've remembered I'm okay,
And I wrote myself this poem.

Lonely

I'm in a permanent state of loneliness,
It seems to be my biggest fear.
I'm by myself so I'm anxious,
That I'll never have anyone near.

I'm in a permanent state of loneliness,
It haunts my every waking day.
I'm by myself so I'm depressed,
Everyone I love is so far away.

I'm in a permanent state of loneliness,
This house makes me feel alone.
I'm by myself so I'm worried,
That I'll never feel safe in my home.

I'm in a permanent state of loneliness,
It's my affliction for being alive,
I'm by myself so I'm hurting,
With just me, I'll never survive.

I'm in a permanent state of loneliness,
I'm begging for someone to help.
I'm by myself so I feel exhausted,
I don't want to be by myself.

Mirrors

Say Hello! to the person in the mirror,
A ‘hello’ and ‘how to you do’,
Is that your own face there looking back at you,
‘I’m fine’, it says and ‘how are you’?

I’m alright, person in the mirror,
I’m managing somehow, getting by,
But I don’t understand dear person,
Why do you look like you want to cry?

‘Cause I do,’ says the person that’s standing there,
‘I do and I know you do too,’
Yeah I guess when I think about it mirror person,
I do want to cry. That is true.

I suppose I had hoped, mirror me,
That it wouldn’t be so obvious how I feel,
Cause I thought I’d been managing to hide it,
But if I see it on you, is it real?

‘It’s alright,’ the mirror person tells me,
‘It’s all going to end up okay,
Just pull yourself together and get on it with it,
Just make it to the end of the day.’

I’ll do as you said mirror me, I will,
I’ll manage to smile and be well
But it’s proving quite hard to be happy right
now,
But that’s a secret I know you won’t tell.

Clothes

I sorted my clothes yesterday into neat little
piles,
T-shirts and jumpers of all types and styles.
Dresses and shoes are all sorted and neat.
Until I had to move it all and I made it
incomplete.
So I moved all my t-shirts, the old and the new,
The trousers and leggings I moved them all too.
Then when I had finished, when it was done,
I found another suitcase, and realised I had just
begun.

Keys

I'm a key collector, a gatherer, a wrangler,
I grab all I can, I'm a key scavenger.
Whenever I go someplace, people all say,
We could hear that girl coming from a mile
away.

The first key I have is the key to my parent's,
The place where I grew up, so of course that
makes sense,
To have a key for there, my access is free,
I can always go home, yes that's guaranteed.

The next key I have is the key to my work,
It's boring, no keyrings, no excitement, no
quirks.
I don't even look at it, don't spare a thought,
It's just on my keyring, another one I've got.

Now keyrings, those I have plenty galore,
Exciting baubles and bits, I've always got more.
I love to collect them, it makes me so pleased,
To have all of my memories right there on my
keys.

Now lastly, this key here, well it's brand new,

The key to my new home has been added too.
My collection for now, at last is complete,
That is, till I find a new keyring next week!

A love letter to Paint

When I think about it,
Paint is quite nice.
It can be quite a mess.
It can be precise.

Paint covers everything,
It covers my face,
But I also quite enjoy,
How it covers my mistakes.

It can be relaxing,
It can be quite upsetting.
I'm up and I'm down,
When I spend my day painting.

And just like my brush,
I can't really get clean.
That's just how painting is,
It's never pristine.

Painting is messy,
Painting is tough,
Painting is difficult,
Painting is rough.

But painting is happy,
Helps the place feel done.
Painting is colourful,
It can even be fun.

So I’m starting to learn,
Yes I’m starting to see,
That mess is alright,
That I can let the mess be.

Cause mess can be fun,
Mess can be freeing,
Mess is just life,
Mess is just being.

What makes a home, I wonder? Part 2

I'm looking back through all that I've been through,
And wondering have I done all that I could do?
Have I earned the title of complete?

Cause I still have bare walls, and empty blank spaces,
I still have untidy and incomplete places,
But the end of the story is here?

So I guess what I'm asking, what I need to know,
Is have I completed what I needed to so,
That I could say I now have a home.

My walls now have pictures, there are smiling faces,
That show happier times and wonderful places,
And just looking at them makes me happy.

My rooms now have colour; bright and cheerful,
Yellow and blues that make me feel gleeful,
And help me to feel at peace.

Yet I still haven't finished, I've still more to do,
But I've accepted that for now I am happy too.
I can continue at my own pace.

So is this being an adult, is that where I am?
Some things are perfect and others are a sham.
I've still got a to-do list that won't stop growing.

Yet I don't really mind, I'm not really worried,
That I still have plenty to do and my mind still is whirring,
Because I know just how much further I already am.

Yes what I have learned through this whole scenario,
Is how to keep going when it seems impossible,
To pull yourself up and carry on.

Cause everything 'broken', everything 'ruined',
Can just be picked up, can be bought anew and,
Nothing is incapable of improvement.

What I have learned, what I've impressed myself with,
Is how I kept going, how I found a new strength,
Which I didn't even know I had.

Because yes it was hard, and yes I was tired,
And yes there were days when I felt uninspired,
But I managed to pull myself together.

And my family and friends, though they could leave me weary,
I am so grateful that they did not abandon me,
They helped me when I needed it most.

And what stands out in this whole challenge?
What is the most important part now and,
What am I proudest of?

Well I'll say what it is and I'll try to be modest,
But I'm most proud of myself if I'm being quite honest.
Cause I did it and that is amazing.

At the end of the day, I made this place my own,
Without me, this house could not be a home,
It's true that I was the key ingredient.

So what makes a home, I wonder?
Is it the feeling of comfort that I've now discovered,
A place where I am most myself.

Cause this house, though I'll admit it's still a big
mess,
Has now become my safety, my own little nest,
My house has become my home.

www.ingramcontent.com/pod-product-compliance
Lightning Source LLC
Chambersburg PA
CBHW051740130826
49812CB00033B/944
* 9 7 8 9 3 9 5 7 8 4 9 5 5 *